Kaneland Middle School
1N137 Meredith Rd.
Maple Park, IL 60151

Reading Essentials
in Science

THE HUMAN BODY

The Respiratory System

SUSAN GLASS

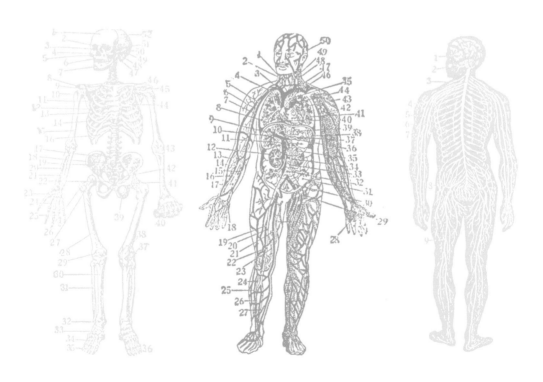

PERFECTION LEARNING®

Editorial Director:	Susan C. Thies
Editor:	Mary L. Bush
Design Director:	Randy Messer
Book Design:	Brianne Osborn
	Emily J. Greazel
Cover Design:	Michael A. Aspengren

A special thanks to the following for their scientific review of the book:

Paul Pistek, Instructor of Biological Sciences, North Iowa Area Community College

Jeffrey Bush, Field Engineer, Vessco, Inc.

Perfection Learning® Corporation
1000 North Second Avenue, P.O. Box 500
Logan, Iowa 51546-0500.
Phone: 1-800-831-4190
Fax: 1-800-543-2745
perfectionlearning.com

2 3 4 5 6 7 PP 09 08 07 06 05 04
ISBN 0-7891-6074-9

Contents

Introduction

Relax and take a deep breath. Feel that fresh air flowing in through your nose and down your throat. Notice your chest rise as the air fills up your lungs. Hold your breath for a second. Now breathe all that air out slowly.

Imagine if you had to think that hard about each breath you took. Could you get anything else done? Luckily, you don't have to think about breathing. Your body does it automatically.

Now take a deep breath again. Hold your breath for as long as possible. Time yourself. Can you last for 30, 40, or even 60 seconds? Has a minute ever lasted so long? Are your lungs screaming for air? When it's more than you can take, let go and breathe again. Perhaps you're more thankful now than ever for the air around you and the ability to breathe it in.

You started life with your first breath, and you'll end it with your last one. You breathe 24 hours a day, 7 days a week. You breathe when you're awake and when you're asleep. You breathe when you think about it and even when you don't. Amazing, isn't it?

The respiratory system is made up of the body parts that work together to make you a living, breathing wonder. So take another deep breath, and let's check it out!

CHAPTER 1

Oh, That Oxygen!

You are surrounded by air. This tasteless, odorless, invisible mixture of gases gives you life.

Almost four-fifths (78 percent) of the air you breathe is a gas called *nitrogen*. Your body doesn't use nitrogen. You just inhale it and then exhale it without using it. Other gases, such as **carbon dioxide**, argon, and others, make up to about 1 percent of air. The mystery gas that is left is the one that your body depends on 24 hours a day—**oxygen**. Oxygen makes up only about one-fifth (21 percent) of the air, but it is essential for human life.

A Lot of Oxygen!

A newborn baby takes about 40 breaths per minute. A one-year-old child slows down to about 24 breaths a minute. Adults average between 10 and 14 breaths per minute. Even though adults breathe more slowly than kids, their bigger lungs take in more air with each breath. An adult takes in around 2 gallons of air each minute. That adds up to about 3000 gallons a day or around 1,095,000 gallons a year.

After two minutes without oxygen, your body's **cells** are damaged. After four minutes, the cells—and you—start to die. Why is oxygen so important?

You are built out of billions of tiny cells. Each of these cells has a special job in your body. All of these cells use oxygen to change the food you eat into energy they can use. The cells need a constant supply of energy to keep your body moving, growing, and thinking.

Oxidation

How do your cells use oxygen to get energy? They use a process called *oxidation*.

Your body takes in oxygen from the air. Your blood picks up the oxygen and takes it to the billions of cells in your body. There, **nutrients** from the food you eat combine with the oxygen. This meeting is oxidation.

Oxidation in your cells releases energy. Your body uses this energy to move, stay warm, grow, and do the jobs necessary to stay alive, such as breathing and pumping your heart.

The faster your body uses energy, the more oxygen it needs to take in. When you exercise hard, your breathing rate, or speed, can rise to as much as 100 times per minute! You take bigger breaths to refuel with oxygen and replace the energy supply you're using.

Try This!

Time yourself for a minute while sitting still or lying down to see how many times you breathe in a minute while resting. Don't force your breathing. Breathe at a normal rate. Record your breathing rate.

Now jog in place for one minute. Then immediately time your breathing rate for a minute. How do the two times compare?

Try different kinds of activities (reading, writing, walking, dancing, etc.). How does each activity change your breathing rate? Make a chart of your rates.

Oxidation in the body is similar to oxidation in a fire. Imagine a campfire. Oxygen from the air combines with fuel to produce energy for the fire. But what happens when you throw dirt on the fire or cover it up? No more s'mores! The oxygen supply is cut off, and the fire goes out. The same happens when your oxygen supply is cut off. You can't continue making energy for your cells, so you begin dying just like the fire.

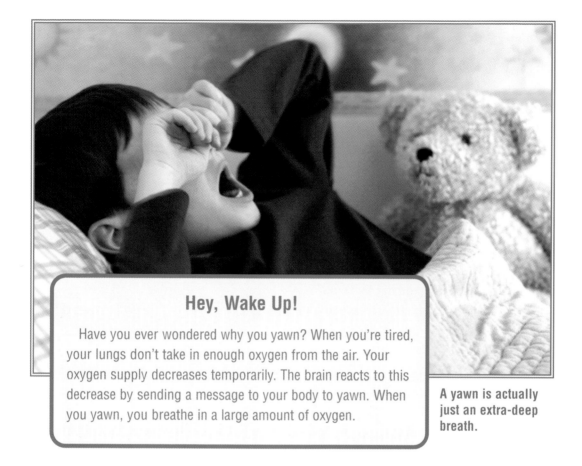

Hey, Wake Up!

Have you ever wondered why you yawn? When you're tired, your lungs don't take in enough oxygen from the air. Your oxygen supply decreases temporarily. The brain reacts to this decrease by sending a message to your body to yawn. When you yawn, you breathe in a large amount of oxygen.

A yawn is actually just an extra-deep breath.

The Exchange

When your cells oxidize food, oxygen gets used up and carbon dioxide is created. Your body can't use this carbon dioxide. It's a waste product that your body needs to get rid of.

The air you breathe in is 21 percent oxygen. The air you breathe out after oxidation is only about 16 percent oxygen. What happened to the other 5 percent? Your lungs snagged it for your cells.

In turn, your lungs "emptied the trash" by exhaling carbon dioxide into the air. The air you breathe in has less than 1 percent carbon dioxide. The air you breathe out has about 4 percent carbon dioxide.

Try This!

Try this experiment to prove that your lungs take oxygen out of the air. You will need a glass jar, a candle small enough to fit inside the jar, some matches or other fire source, a watch or clock, and adult supervision.

Light the candle (or have the adult light it). Cover the candle with the jar. Start timing as soon as you cover the candle. What happens? When the flame dies out because the oxygen in the jar was cut off, record the time.

Uncover the candle and light it again. Then blow several breaths into the jar. Cover the end with your hand in between breaths to keep the exhaled air inside. Now cover the candle with the jar. Time how long it takes for the flame to go out this time.

Did it take more or less time than the first time? It should take less time, because there was less oxygen in the jar after you blew into it.

Just like other muscles in your body, your breathing muscles need workouts to stay strong.

Remember how you breathe faster when exercising to take in more oxygen? You also breathe more during exercise to get rid of carbon dioxide. The faster your cells make and use energy, the faster carbon dioxide is produced. Your body needs to breathe faster to exhale the extra carbon dioxide.

Breathing is an even exchange. Inhaling provides needed oxygen, and exhaling gets rid of unnecessary carbon dioxide. So with each breath you take, you're getting exactly what you need.

CHAPTER 2

The Respiratory System

Why is your breathing system called the *respiratory system*? The word *respiration* has several meanings. *Respiration* can mean all the things your body does to get oxygen to the cells and to get rid of carbon dioxide. It can also be used in talking about breathing. For example, your respiration rate is your breathing rate. Both are a measure of how fast you breathe. Sometimes scientists use the word *respiration* to discuss what goes on in the cells when energy is released from food.

All of these definitions have something to do with breathing. So the *respiratory* system is the breathing system that brings oxygen into the body and gets rid of carbon dioxide.

The respiratory system is important to all of the body systems. Each of these other systems needs oxygen so the cells can perform their jobs. But the respiratory system works most closely with the circulatory system. These two systems work together to get oxygen to all of the cells. Your circulatory system consists of your heart, **blood vessels**, and blood. The heart pumps blood through the vessels to all the cells in your body. The blood loads up with oxygen in the lungs to deliver it throughout your body. At the same time, it picks up carbon dioxide at the cells and returns it to the lungs. The lungs then get rid of the carbon dioxide. These two systems depend on each other to keep the flow of oxygen and carbon dioxide moving through your body.

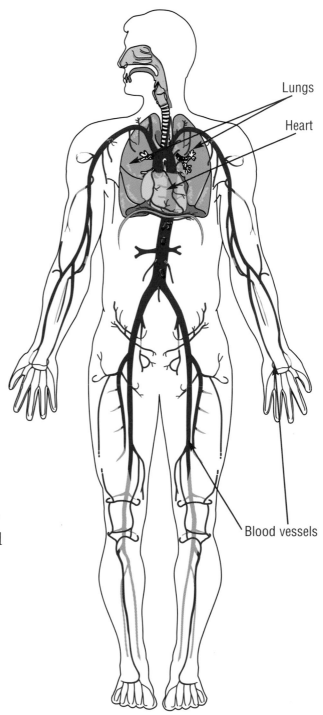

Lungs

Heart

Blood vessels

To Think About It or Not to Think About It

Breathing is both a voluntary and involuntary process. *Voluntary* means that you can make choices about your breathing. You can choose to take quick, short breaths. You can choose to take deep, slow breaths. You can even choose to hold your breath (at least for a while).

Most of the time, though, you don't think about breathing. It is involuntary. It happens automatically without thought or choice.

The respiratory center in your **brain stem** controls involuntary breathing. When there is too much carbon dioxide in your blood, the nerve cells in the respiratory center send signals to the breathing muscles to speed up. If you hold your breath too long, the respiratory center in the brain will command you to breathe again. If you choose to ignore this command, you will eventually faint and start to breathe automatically again.

The respiratory center in your brain stem also controls your rate, or speed, of breathing. It makes sure that you have just the right amount of oxygen to provide energy for whatever you're doing—sleeping, singing, rock climbing, etc. That is why you huff and you puff like the big bad wolf when you work or play hard and breathe deeply and calmly when relaxing.

From First to Last Breath

Respiration, or breathing, is the key to life. When you were born, everyone breathed a sigh of relief when you took your first breath. Your respiratory system has worked hard every minute of your life since then to keep supplying you with the oxygen you need.

Come On In
The Mouth and Nose

The respiratory system's main parts are the nose, the mouth, the **trachea**, the lungs, and the diaphragm. Each part plays an important role in respiration.

Your nose is the in and out door for your respiratory system. Sometimes your mouth helps too. Think about how miserable you would be with a stuffed-up nose if your mouth couldn't help out with breathing!

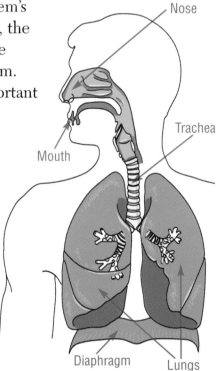

Nose

Trachea

Mouth

Diaphragm

Lungs

Your nose and mouth are actually connected inside. Have you ever laughed with a mouthful of liquid that shot up your nose? Now you know why.

Try breathing in through your nose and out through your mouth. Now try breathing in through your mouth and out through your nose. Imagine the air passing through the connecting tube inside.

The Nose Knows How to Breathe

Even though you can breathe through your mouth, your nose is the part really made for breathing. Your nose holes are called *nostrils*. Air enters your respiratory system through the nostrils.

Behind the nose is the nasal cavity. *Nasal* means having to do with the nose. The nasal cavity is a hollow space that the air moves through. Air flows through the curves in the nasal cavity. These pathways are called the *nasal passages*.

Nasal cavity

The nose and nasal cavity have special equipment to clean, warm, and moisten the incoming air. Nose hairs and **mucus** are two helpful respiratory tools. Your mouth doesn't have these special features. Aren't you glad? Just thinking about mouth hairs and mouth mucus is enough to make you gag. (The mouth does, however, have saliva, which moistens the air.)

What do nose hairs do? They catch dust, **pollen**, smoke, bugs, or other particles that get sucked into your nose. The hairs keep all this dirty stuff from entering your respiratory system.

Nostrils or Nares?

Scientists call your nostrils the *external nares*. So if anyone ever catches you with a finger up your nose, just tell them that you're checking your external nares. If nothing else, it may make them forget what you were doing!

Some of the particles get stuck in the mucus that lines the nostrils and nasal cavity. Mucus is a slippery, slimy liquid that moistens and cleans the nasal passages. Normally it is clear and colorless. Mucus is good at catching germs that float in the air as well as other particles that would be bad for the lungs.

Anyone Have a Kleenex?

If trapped particles or germs irritate your nose, your body reacts by blasting them out with a sneeze. When you sneeze, air shoots out of your nose faster than 90 miles an hour. Just one sneeze can spray 100,000 droplets of mucus and germs into the air. If a person nearby inhales some of these droplets, he or she gets your germs. That's why it's a good idea to cover your mouth when you sneeze.

The nasal cavity is also lined with lots of little blood vessels called *capillaries*. These vessels are full of warm blood. The capillaries act as tiny heaters that warm the incoming air. Heat from capillaries in the nose lining warms the air to near body temperature. In cold weather, if the air doesn't get warmed enough before it hits your lungs, your chest will ache.

Some of the water in the mucus that lines the nasal cavity **evaporates** into the incoming air. This makes the air going to the lungs moist. Dry air can dry out the delicate **tissues** in the lungs.

Air that is inhaled travels through the curvy nasal passages. This pathway also helps prepare the air for its respiratory journey. The curves in the passages slow the air down and give the body more time to warm, clean, and moisten the air before it heads down the throat.

Holes in Your Head

The nasal cavity is surrounded by sinuses. Sinuses are hollow spaces in the skull. Yes, you really do have holes in your head! Actually you have eight holes—four pairs of sinuses—in your head. They are located on the sides of your nose, behind and between your eyes, in your forehead, and at the back of your nose.

Sinuses make your head lighter. This means you can hold your head up and keep it balanced. Otherwise it might be too heavy.

Sinuses also moisturize the air and make mucus to help out your nasal cavity. Normally, extra mucus from the sinuses slides down the back of your nose to your throat. However, when your sinuses are infected, the mucus doesn't flow out. It blocks up your sinuses. This can cause a stuffy nose and pain and pressure in your head and face.

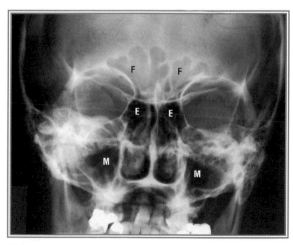

This X ray shows three pairs of sinuses. F shows the sinuses in the forehead, E shows those between and behind the eyes, and M indicates those on either side of the nose.

CHAPTER 4

Working Its Way Down the Windpipe

The moist, warm, clean air travels from your nose down into your throat. There it meets a fork in the road. One path leads to the rest of the respiratory system. The other one leads to the stomach and the digestive system. Have you ever gulped down air into your stomach and then had to burp to get it back out? Or have you ever had food go down the "wrong tube" so you had to cough it back up? These things happen when your air or food takes the wrong path by accident. But when things work as they should, traffic gets directed by a little flap called the *epiglottis*.

The epiglottis is open most of the time since you are always breathing. An open flap directs air to the trachea, or windpipe, and down to the lungs. It's normally open because you don't swallow as often as you breathe.

Believe it or not, though, on an average day, you swallow 1000 times or more. When you swallow, the epiglottis flap closes. This shuts off the trachea, so the food or saliva moves down the food tube called the *esophagus.*

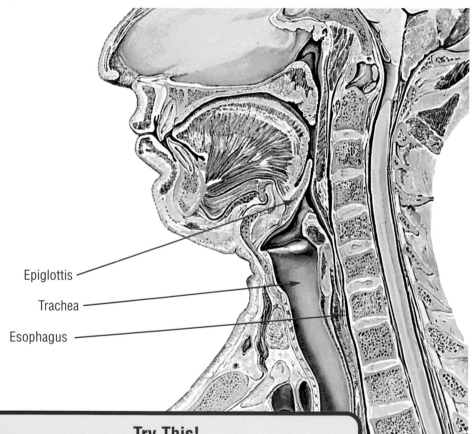

Epiglottis

Trachea

Esophagus

Try This!

Try breathing and swallowing at the same time. Can you do it? No, you can't. Since your epiglottis shuts off either the esophagus or the trachea, you can't breathe and swallow at the same time.

The Trachea (Otherwise Known as the Windpipe)

Do you know how to find your trachea? Put your fingers on the bump on the front of your throat. Keep your fingers on it while you swallow. Can you feel it move up and down? That bump is your larynx, or voice box. Inside it are the vocal cords that vibrate, or move back and forth, to make sound so you can speak, sing, yell, or scream. The larynx is attached to the top end of the trachea.

The epiglottis is attached to the top of the larynx. When you breathe, the epiglottis opens, allowing the air to move through the larynx into the trachea.

Rub your fingers on your lower throat. Can you feel the ridges? If not, try tilting your head back. The ridges are cartilage rings that partially encircle and protect your trachea. Cartilage is the tough but bendable material that you can feel in your ears and at the end of your nose. The cartilage rings that go around your trachea keep it from closing off when it gets bent. You can bend your neck in any direction and the trachea will not close off. The air can always get through. The rings also keep your windpipe from collapsing as the air moves in and out and the lungs and esophagus press on it.

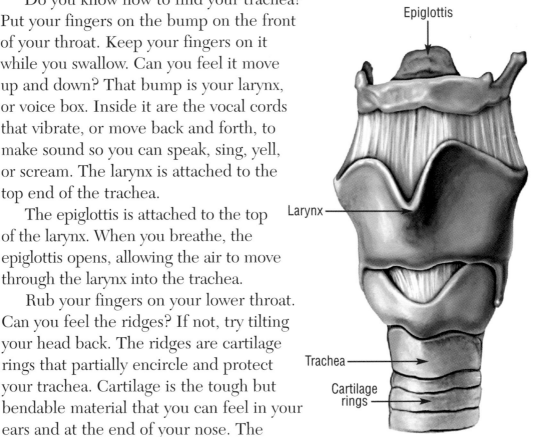

Epiglottis

Larynx

Trachea

Cartilage rings

Not a Complete Circle

The cartilage rings don't go all the way around the windpipe. There is no cartilage in the back next to the esophagus. This makes room for your food pipe to expand when you swallow, so food doesn't get stuck.

When Food Goes Down the Wrong Tube

Normally when you swallow, the larynx moves upward and the epiglottis tips to close off the opening to the windpipe. The food then moves down the esophagus, which is hiding behind the windpipe.

But what happens when food accidentally slips past the epiglottis into the windpipe? Food or liquid in the windpipe will irritate the trachea, causing you to cough. When you cough, your chest **contracts** and air rushes up. The air flies out of your mouth at speeds over 300 miles per hour. Any objects in the path are blasted out of the way.

Coughing usually clears most things out of the respiratory airways. However, once in a while, someone cannot cough up the object blocking the trachea. Sometimes the airway is completely blocked, and no air can pass through. Without air, there's no respiration, or breathing. What should you do then?

Stop Coughing Please!

Have you ever sat next to someone with a cough and been irritated by the rough, barking sound? Do you know what makes that sound? When the air rushes up your trachea, it rattles your vocal cords. This makes that annoying coughing sound.

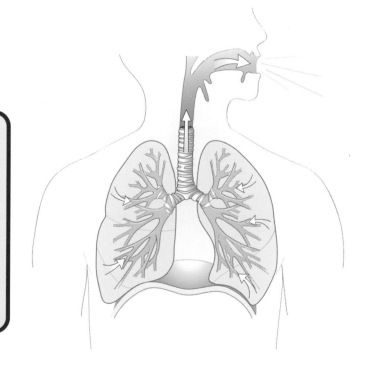

Choking, caused by food or some other foreign object in the windpipe, is responsible for more than 3000 deaths a year in the United States. This makes coughing one of the body's best defense mechanisms.

The best thing to do is follow a method developed by Dr. Henry Heimlich. It's called the Heimlich maneuver. This procedure involves squeezing the choking person in the correct place in order to force the object out of the trachea. The Heimlich maneuver should never be used by someone who hasn't been trained in the procedure as it can cause more harm if done incorrectly.

The Heimlich Manuever

1. Stand behind the choking person. Make a fist and place your thumb on the inside next to the person's body.

3. With your thumb next to the choking person's abdomen, wrap your other arm around the person and hold your fist with the other hand.

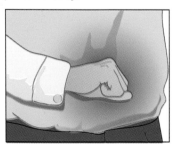

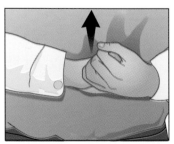

2. Place your fist below the person's rib cage and in the center of the body.

4. Give the person a fast and forceful thrust upward. Continue until the item is dislodged from the person's throat.

Lungs of Life

The trachea runs from your neck down into your chest. There it branches into two tubes—the right **bronchus** and the left bronchus. Each of these bronchi leads to a lung.

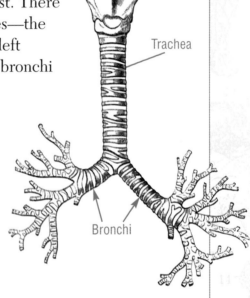

Trachea

Bronchi

One or More Than One?

Bronchi is the plural form of *bronchus*. One tube is a bronchus. Both tubes are bronchi.

Load Up on Lung Facts

Adult lungs are each about the size of a football. They are light enough to float on water. Each lung weighs about two pounds when it is full of air. When the lungs are inflated, or full of air, they fill the chest entirely—all the way up to the shoulders.

Healthy lungs are a pale pink color. Each lung is covered by pleural membranes. These membranes are two thin, slippery layers separated by a fluid. This fluid keeps lung movements smooth and easy.

The lungs are not the same size. The right lung is a bit bigger. The left lung is smaller to make room for your heart.

Each lung is divided into sections, or lobes. The right lung has three lobes—the upper, middle, and lower lobes. The left lung has just an upper and lower lobe.

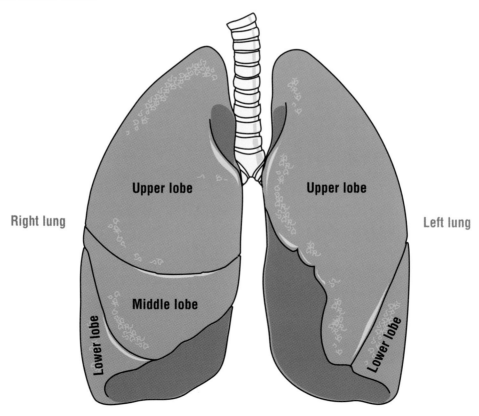

Trees in the Lungs

Inside each lung, the two bronchi branch into smaller and smaller bronchial tubes. These tubes look like the branches of an upside-down tree with the trachea as the trunk. It is even called the *bronchial tree*. The smallest branches are **bronchioles**.

The bronchioles end at very tiny air sacs, or **alveoli**. Alveoli cluster around the end of each bronchiole like a bunch of miniature grapes. An average person's lungs have about 600 million alveoli. These tiny air sacs give lungs their spongelike quality. Your lungs can soak up oxygen just like a sponge soaks up water.

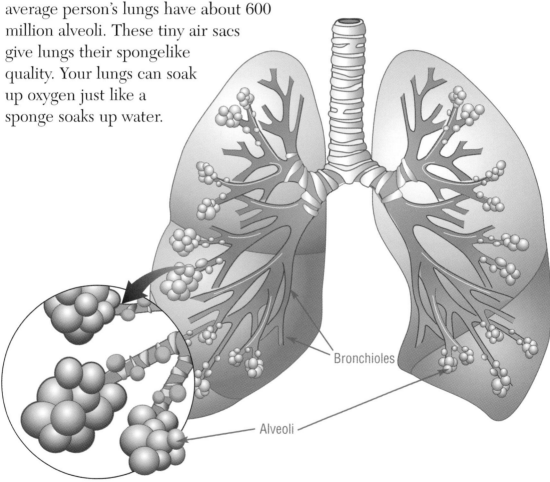

Bronchioles

Alveoli

Made for Speed

Speed is important to the respiratory system. An adult has about one quart of oxygen available in his or her blood at any one time. When the body's cells need oxygen, they need it immediately. If you ran the 100-yard dash, your body would use up about seven quarts of oxygen in the time it took to run the race. Fast, deep breathing sucks extra oxygen into the body. The bronchial tree spreads it out in the lungs in seconds.

When you think of lungs, do you picture flat air bags that fill up with air and then **deflate**? If this were true, your lungs wouldn't have enough surface area for oxygen and carbon dioxide to move in and out fast enough. The balloon shape of the alveoli create much more space for this exchange.

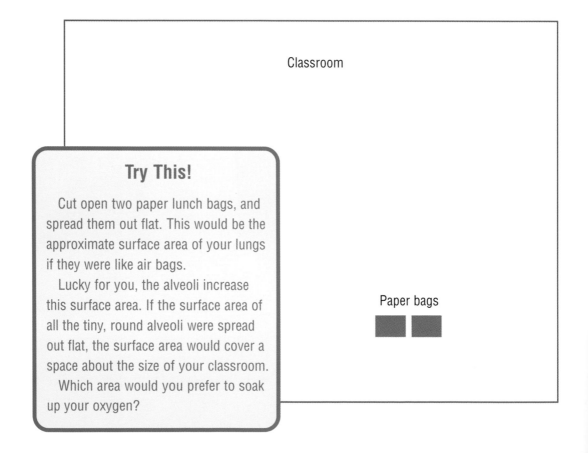

Classroom

Paper bags

Try This!

Cut open two paper lunch bags, and spread them out flat. This would be the approximate surface area of your lungs if they were like air bags.

Lucky for you, the alveoli increase this surface area. If the surface area of all the tiny, round alveoli were spread out flat, the surface area would cover a space about the size of your classroom.

Which area would you prefer to soak up your oxygen?

Lung capacity is affected by physical exercise. People who are physically active usually have a larger lung capacity than those who aren't active.

Oxygen enters your blood through tiny blood vessels called capillaries. These capillaries surround the alveoli, ready to carry out gas exchange. Carbon dioxide also exits your blood through these vessels. Capillaries are so small that their walls are only one cell thick. It's easy for oxygen and carbon dioxide to pass right through these walls. Your blood meets the air in the capillaries in the lungs. If lungs were like bags, there wouldn't be enough surface area inside covered with capillaries to do the job. Instead, the balloon-shaped alveoli provide more space for capillaries. Each lung is like a sponge with about 300 million tiny bubbles inside.

Unbelievably Large Lungs!

The surface area of the lungs is about 25 times larger than the surface area of the skin.

The blood that enters the lungs' capillaries has already traveled around the body delivering oxygen to needy cells. When it reaches the lungs, the blood is very low on oxygen. It needs a fast fill-up. The lungs supply the blood with fresh oxygen almost instantly. Within one second of arriving in the lungs, the blood is full of oxygen and ready to return to the rest of the body.

Try This!

How much air can your lungs hold? Use a balloon to find out. Take a deep breath and blow as much air as you can in one breath into the balloon. Check out the size of the balloon. Let the air out of the balloon and try again. Is the balloon bigger or smaller? Try a few more times and compare. If you want to be really accurate, use a measuring tape to measure the distance around the center, or circumference, of the balloon each time.

Have a contest to see whose lungs can hold the most air. Grab a few of your classmates and a balloon for each one. See who can blow up the largest balloon using only one breath. The winner really is "full of hot air"!

Protection for the Lungs

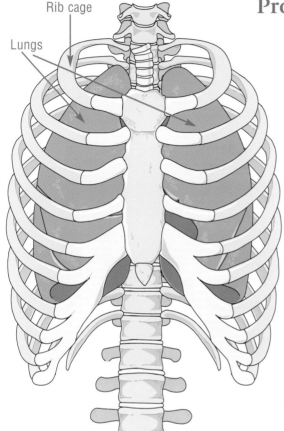

Rib cage

Lungs

Lungs are very delicate, so they are well protected. They are shielded on the outside by a cage made of rib bones. It is called the *rib cage*. These hard bones protect your lungs from being punctured, or ripped, if you're hit hard in the chest.

Your lungs also need protection on the inside. Often the air you breathe is too dirty, too dry, or too cold for the fragile alveoli. Air has to be filtered, moistened, and warmed before it ever reaches the lungs. Otherwise the thin alveoli can get irritated, torn, or dried out.

Luckily, mighty mucus is on the job. The nose, throat, trachea, bronchi, and bronchioles are all lined with mucus. It's disgusting stuff, but it's awfully good at its job. Dirt or dust in the respiratory path sticks to this mucus so it can't harm the lungs.

These same passageways are also lined with cilia. Cilia are tiny hairlike sweepers. They whip and wave around about ten times a second. That's about 36,000 times every hour. How many times is that in a day?

How Many Sweepers?

One tiny hairlike sweeper is a *cilium*. More than one of these waving hairs are *cilia*.

Outdoor air pollutants, such as those released into the air by factories, harm fragile lung tissues and threaten the health of people breathing the air.

Cilia push dirt and dust toward your mouth. The cilia in the nasal passages wave down toward the mouth. The cilia in the trachea and lungs wave upward. Billions and billions of cilia wave back and forth like cornstalks in the wind. They create a sort of mucus current that travels almost half an inch each minute. Smoke, pollen, dirt, germs, and other harmful particles get stuck in the sticky mucus along the way. They get pushed up with the mucus back to your throat. Then you swallow them. Sounds yummy, doesn't it?

The good news is that these particles are no match for the stomach-acid bath that awaits them at the end of a swallow. Your digestive system helps get rid of the harmful substances in your respiratory system. It's like a buddy system in your body systems!

If any harmful intruders make it past all the respiratory system's cilia and mucus defenders, they still have to face the white cells in the alveoli called *macrophages*. These cells act like police officers on patrol. They wait for harmful substances and then wrap their jellylike bodies around them and eat them.

Mucus, cilia, and macrophages work together to make sure your lungs stay healthy. You breathe in dust, dirt, and germs with almost every breath, so your lungs' defenders keep very busy.

A Mighty Muscle—The Diaphragm

Lungs are speedy, stretchy, and spongy. But surprisingly, they are completely unable to move by themselves. So how do they expand (grow larger) and contract (shrink)? Muscles do all the work!

Take a deep breath. What happens to your chest when you breathe in? It expands because it fills with air, right? Actually, it's the other way around. Your chest fills with air because it expands.

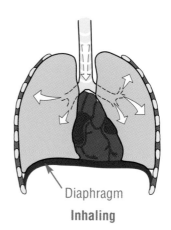

Inhaling

When you inhale, rib muscles pull the ribs up and out so your chest expands. At the same time, the dome-shaped muscle under your lungs flattens out. This muscle is the **diaphragm**. The diaphragm does most of the work in breathing. The incoming air does not make the chest spread out. The chest expands first, and then the air rushes in. When the rib and diaphragm muscles relax, the air is squeezed out of the lungs and you exhale.

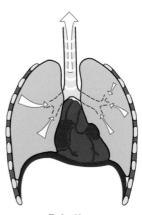

Exhaling

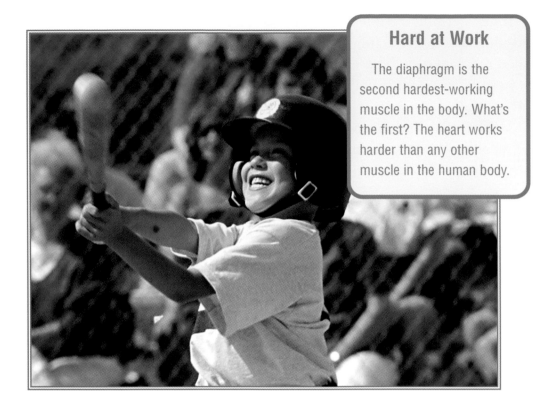

How Do Hiccups Happen?

Hiccups happen when the diaphragm jerks suddenly. The muscle flattens quickly, and air rushes in. The epiglottis snaps shut to stop the sudden rush of air through the vocal cords. This causes the "hic" sound and the jerking motion you get when the hiccup pops out.

Why do you hiccup? It may be that your diaphragm has been irritated or the nerves that control your diaphragm aren't working properly. The stomach often seems to be responsible for hiccups. Eating too fast or eating certain foods may trigger hiccups. Even smelling harmful fumes may bring on an annoying round of hiccups.

Most hiccups last for a few minutes at most. But there have been cases of people having hiccups that go on for years! Some "cures" for hiccups include holding your breath and swallowing, breathing into a paper bag, putting sugar under your tongue, or being scared by someone or something. What works for you?

CHAPTER 6

Respiratory Risks

A healthy respiratory system is an efficient machine that keeps you breathing easily day and night. But sometimes germs, diseases, and harmful substances can cause temporary or permanent changes in the way your system works. They put your respiratory system at risk.

Colds and More

Almost everyone has had a cold sometime in his or her life. We're all familiar with the coughing, sneezing, and runny nose that make our days miserable and our nights sleepless. But what is a cold? A cold is an infection caused by a virus. Viruses are germs that invade your body. Your body's defense system springs into action to fight and destroy these harmful invaders. That's why a cold normally only lasts a few days.

Cold viruses are usually in the upper respiratory system (nose and throat). Sometimes, though, an infection spreads to or develops in the lungs. Bronchitis or pneumonia are two infections that affect the lungs. In addition to cold symptoms, these illnesses can include deep coughing, chest pain, fever, and difficulty breathing.

Allergies

Sometimes cold symptoms appear and it isn't a cold at all. It's allergies. How can you tell if it's a cold or allergies? If the coughing, sneezing, and runny nose last for more than a couple of weeks, it might be an allergy. If your nose and eyes itch, it could be an allergy. Colds won't usually make you itchy. Also, if you have a cold, the mucus in your nose is normally yellowish and thick. With an allergy, the mucus is clear.

So what is an allergy? An allergy is a body's overreaction to a harmless substance. The body's defense system is always ready to attack harmful substances. But sometimes this defense system reacts to substances that aren't normally harmful. It acts as though these substances are going to hurt the body and begins to destroy them.

Anything that causes an allergy is called an *allergen*. Your body's immune system fights invading germs. When you have an allergy, your body treats allergens as if they are harmful invading germs. It's like a false alarm. Your immune system begins to break down the allergens in your tissues and blood cells. The cells then release chemicals that cause allergy symptoms.

Defending Your Body

You are constantly breathing in dirt and germs. What protects your body against these unhealthy substances? The immune system is your body's defense system. The immune system defends your body by attacking harmful substances and destroying them.

One in five Americans has allergies. Allergies can be inherited. If one parent has an allergy, a child has a one in three chance of having one. If both parents have allergies, chances are seven out of ten that their child will have them too. Although allergies run in families, different family members may be allergic to different things.

Allergies that trouble your respiratory system can be caused by many things. Some people are allergic to dust mites. Dust mites are tiny bugs that live in dust. They eat the flakes of dead skin that humans shed all the time. Dust mites can live in carpets, bedding, and stuffed animals.

Have you or someone you know ever wanted a cat or dog but couldn't get one because someone in the family has allergies? Animal dander is another common allergen. Dander is tiny bits of skin from furry animals. About ten million Americans are allergic to cat dander alone. Some people are also allergic to the feathers, fur, or saliva of certain animals.

Studies have shown that children who live with pets in their home during the first year of life are less likely to develop pet allergies or other common allergies as well.

The king of all allergens, however, is pollen. Pollen is a fine, yellowish powder in flowering plants. When these plants release their pollen into the air, the traveling powder causes allergies to act up. This usually happens in summer or fall. Seasonal pollen allergies are often called *hay fever*.

Hay fever symptoms affect the nose, eyes, and throat. The **mucous membrane** that lines the nose and nasal cavity becomes inflamed, or swollen. Sneezing and an itchy or runny nose are common. The eyes and throat can also itch and water.

Allergies can be treated with medicines. The best "medicine," however, is to avoid the allergens.

This photograph shows flower pollen from the elder tree magnified 2400 times. The elder tree is a small, unpleasant-smelling tree that grows in many different habitats. Flowers from the elder tree are in herbal medicines used to treat bronchitis, eczema, fever, and sinus problems.

Asthma

Asthma is an illness that causes the bronchioles to become swollen and irritated. These tiny tubes become even narrower. Not enough air passes through the lungs, so breathing is difficult.

Asthma is very common in children. About one out of ten children has an occasional mild attack, or flare-up, of asthma. Many kids outgrow it during their teenage years.

Asthma affects twice as many boys as girls in childhood. But in the teen years, more girls than boys suffer from this illness. By adulthood, the number of men and women with asthma is equal.

Missing School

About one-fourth of school absences are due to asthma.

Most cases of asthma in children and teenagers are due to allergic reactions to pollen, dust mites, and animal dander. But pollution and smoke can also cause problems because people with asthma are more sensitive to things that they inhale.

"Triggers" are things that set off an asthma attack. Cold air, exercise, dust, emotional upsets, infections, and some medications are common triggers.

In between attacks, a person with asthma breathes normally. But during an attack, breathing is like trying to inhale through a straw. Wheezing, or whistling, while breathing is common. The muscle bands around the bronchi and bronchioles start to tighten. The airways get narrower, and breathing becomes more and more difficult. The tubes also start to produce more mucus, which clogs them up.

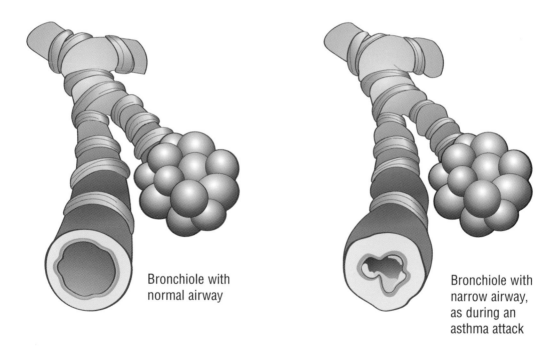

Bronchiole with normal airway

Bronchiole with narrow airway, as during an asthma attack

During an asthma attack, breathing out is actually harder than breathing in.

Asthma attacks can range from mild to severe. In a mild attack, the chest tightens and coughing and wheezing are common. Severe attacks can result in trouble breathing and talking, tight neck muscles, and gray or blue lips and fingernails. Some people suffer from attacks only during hard exercise. Others experience symptoms every day.

Asthma can be managed with medicines. Many kids use inhalers to help them open up their airways when they have an attack. Other medicines are used to reduce swelling and irritation, which prevents attacks. Avoiding triggers helps too.

Inhaler

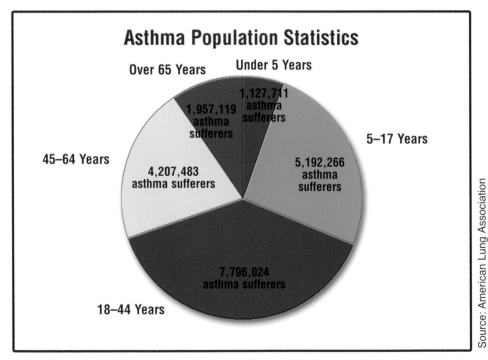

More than 20 million people in the United States suffer from asthma conditions.

Smoking

Smoke is an asthma trigger, but that's only one of the ways it can hurt the respiratory system. Smoking can damage the mouth, throat, and lungs. It can cause cancer and other diseases that can be deadly. A nonsmoker is likely to live up to 15 or 20 years longer than a smoker.

Tobacco smoke contains several harmful substances. The biggest villains are nicotine, carbon monoxide, and tar.

Nicotine acts on the brain, producing the relaxing feeling that smokers experience. The problem is that nicotine is addictive. The body gets hooked on it quickly, and smokers need a steady supply to feel well. Nicotine keeps smokers smoking, which leads to respiratory problems.

Carbon monoxide is a poisonous gas. It can damage the heart and lungs. It robs the body of oxygen. If you smoke, red blood cells that would normally carry oxygen to your cells carry carbon monoxide instead. The heart and lungs have to work harder to get oxygen to the cells.

More than 440,000 people in the United States die each year from cigarette smoking-related illnesses.

Tar is inhaled as a vapor, or gas, into the lungs. There it turns into a thick liquid that clogs airways and kills tiny cilia.

Smoke causes mucus to thicken and clog tiny bronchioles. Smoke also damages or destroys the cilia sweepers that would normally push germs out of the respiratory system. Instead, smokers rid their airways of mucus and germs by coughing. But coughing isn't as effective at removing harmful substances as cilia are. This causes smokers to get sick more often than nonsmokers.

Smoking can damage the alveoli as well. Those tiny and delicate air sacs can lose the ability to stretch and to let oxygen and carbon dioxide through their walls properly. Once the alveoli are damaged, they cannot be repaired.

Smoking is a disaster for your respiratory system. Nine out of ten cases of lung cancer are caused by smoking. Smokers risk getting mouth and throat cancer too.

Scary Statistics

Lung cancer is the leading cause of death due to respiratory disease. Pneumonia is the second cause of death related to respiratory problems.

Secondhand Smoke

Smokers only hurt themselves, right? Wrong! Breathing in smoke from someone else's cigarette can be just as dangerous as smoking your own cigarette.

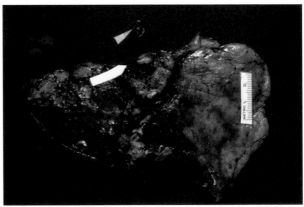

The harmful chemicals in cigarette smoke cause healthy pink lungs to blacken.

This smoke from other people's cigarettes, cigars, or pipes is known as secondhand smoke.

Employees of restaurants and other places where people are allowed to smoke can develop problems similar to smokers. Children who live with adults who smoke suffer from more colds, ear infections, bronchitis, and other respiratory problems such as asthma. Babies of moms who smoke are more likely to be born early, have breathing problems, and be underweight. Studies have even shown that dogs living with smokers are more likely to get lung cancer.

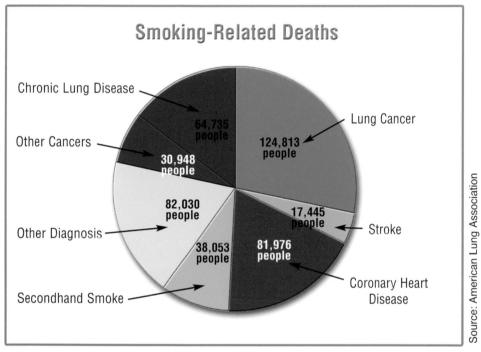

Smoking-Related Deaths

Chronic Lung Disease — 64,735 people

Other Cancers — 30,948 people

Lung Cancer 124,813 people

Other Diagnosis — 82,030 people

Stroke — 17,445 people

Secondhand Smoke — 38,053 people

Coronary Heart Disease — 81,976 people

Source: American Lung Association

Approximately 440,000 people in the United States die each year from diseases related to cigarette smoking.

Better Breathing

Some respiratory problems, such as allergies and asthma, cannot be avoided. But having a healthy lifestyle can lessen the effects of these problems and prevent other respiratory illnesses. It's up to you to keep your nose, mouth, throat, and lungs in good shape for a future of peaceful breathing.

Internet Connections and Related Reading for the Respiratory System

http://kidshealth.org/kid/body/lungs_SW.html
Get a close-up look at the lungs to see where they're located, how they work, and how to protect them.

http://yucky.kids.discovery.com/noflash/body/pg000138.html/
Begin your discovery of the respiratory system with this simple description.

http://vilenski.org/science/humanbody/hb_html/respiratory.html
Review the parts of the respiratory system, and then take a quiz to see what you've learned.

http://www.sk.lung.ca/content.cfm/kids
This Lung Association site explains how and why you breathe and provides a diagram and information on each part of the respiratory system. You can also learn more about lung diseases, such as allergies and asthma.

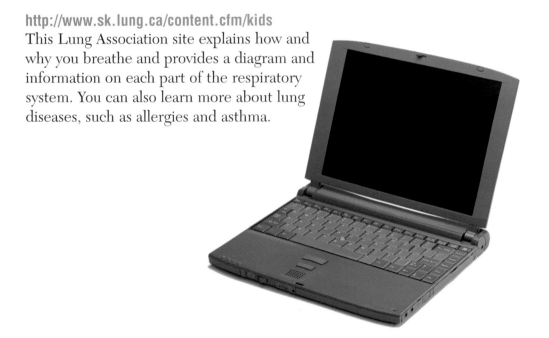

http://hes.ucf.k12.pa.us/gclaypo/
repiratorysys.html
Take a quick tour through the respiratory system, and find out some fun
facts about your amazing breathing machine.

Human Body by Steve Parker. An Eyewitness Book on the human body.
Dorling Kindersley, 1993. [RL 7.7 IL 3–8] (5868906 HB)

•RL = Reading Level
•IL = Interest Level
Perfection Learning's catalog numbers are included for your ordering convenience.
HB indicates hardback.

Glossary

alveoli (al VEE uh leye) tiny air sacs in the lungs

blood vessel (bluhd VES uhl) tube through which blood flows through the body

brain stem (brayn stem) part of the body that connects the brain and spinal cord and controls breathing

bronchiole (BRAHNK ee ohl) small tube in the lungs that carries air to the alveoli (see separate entry for *alveoli*)

bronchus (BRAHNK uhs) tube connecting the trachea and a lung (see separate entry for *trachea*)

carbon dioxide (CAR buhn deye OKS seyed) gas that is exhaled by humans as a waste product

cell (sel) smallest unit of living matter

contracts (kuhn TRAKTS) squeezes together to become smaller

deflate (dee FLAYT) to release or lose air

diaphragm (DEYE uh fram) muscle that moves the lungs

evaporate (ee VAP or ayt) to change from a liquid to a gas

mucous membrane (MYOU kuhs MEM brayn) thin layer of cells in the nose and other parts of the body that produces mucus (see separate entries for *cell* and *mucus*)

mucus (MYOU kuhs) liquid that moistens and cleans the nasal passages

nutrient (NOO tree ent) material that living things need to live and grow

oxygen (OKS uh juhn) gas that human body cells use to change food into energy

pollen (PAH lin) powdery particles of a plant's flower that are used to make new plants

tissue (TISH you) group of similar cells working together (see separate entry for *cell*)

trachea (TRAY kee uh) tube that connects the throat and lungs

Index